JENNIE HALE *is a ceramic artist who lives in Devon. For many years, she has kept a nature diary and in this book she shares a selection of the entries and watercolour drawings from her diary sketchbooks. The result is a charming look at the English countryside in the course of a year.*

Dedication

To Andrew, Jamie and Robyn

Acknowledgements

Throughout my life I have met like-minded people, many of whom have given their time and energy to help me. I am endlessly grateful to all of those people, but especially to my parents Sheila and Ian, who raised a child with a wild and independent spirit and to Andrew, Jamie and Robyn, who have learned to live with the bugs in the fridge and all the strange objects I bring home to draw.

To Peter Newman, my landlord and the owner of the Coryton Estate, for allowing me the run of his land where I find so much that inspires me.

To the late Ruth Murray who always had time to talk about, and let me draw, her beloved Badgers.

To David Measures for writing the foreword to this book and for his encouragement and the knowledge that he gives so happily about painting and wildlife.

To John Walters for our days out in the field painting.

To Alan Reid of the Forestry Commission, for listening to my endless babble about wildlife and for sharing his skill and knowledge.

To the girls and the guys in the D.R.G. Tavistock for sharing our adventures.

To Linda and Sutchinda of A&C Black for believing in this book and working so hard to put it together.

And to all my friends for their help and support with some of my many daft ideas!

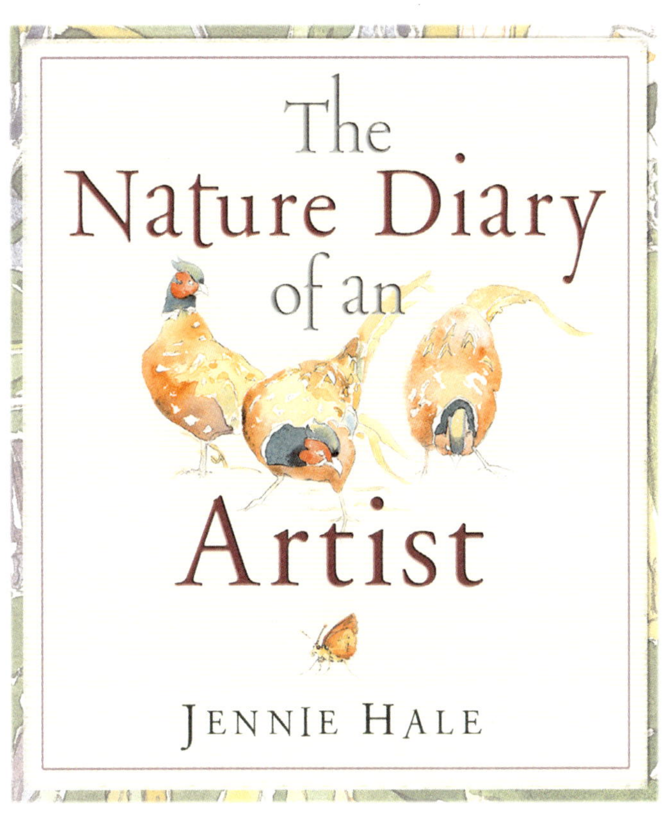

HERBERT PRESS • LONDON

First published in Great Britain 2007
The Herbert Press
an imprint of A&C Black
38 Soho Square
London W1D 3HB

ISBN 978 0 7136 8652 4

A CIP catalogue record for this book is available from
the British Library

Book and cover design by Sutchinda Rangsi Thompson
Printed and bound in China by C&C Offset Printing Co., Ltd.

This book is produced using paper that is made from wood grown in managed, sustainable forests. It is natural, renewable and recyclable. The logging and manufacturing processes conform to the environmental regulations of the country of origin.

Foreword

This book is a delight. Jennie is a find; she is unique among wildlife artists. Her work comes 'fresh as a daisy in spring'. Everyone will be charmed by the simplicity of her captured images of the wild; all done outside on the spot, thereby containing the maximum authenticity. Wildlife, here one moment gone the next, has to be captured in haste; in contrast plant life gives her time to ponder and stay until something satisfies her.

She lives and works as a potter in a beautiful wooded valley on the edge of Dartmoor with her family. It was while foraging to obtain material for her pottery that the nature diary was begun. She has a really good landlord who lets her explore the limits of his ground and is as excited at what she finds and paints as the rest of us. Early morning sees her out with her dog and sketchbook and come darkness she is again accompanied by her faithful shadow, the perfect companion when drawing newts, frogs and toads by torchlight in the woodland pools or bats in addits using a torch on her forehead.

This collection of drawings in a calendar year shows us what Devon has to offer and shows what a glorious county it is. But you don't just go out and bring back a painting – you have to hunt for it. You have to use all your field-craft and even then you can come back without a painting of what you set out to do. Deer, foxes, hares are timorous creatures, and are endowed with the three senses – sight, sound and smell, which are much more acute than ours. Jennie has over the many years gained a lot of field experience in order to bring us so many paintings of these shy mammals. It's not always good weather you need – the worst cold, wind or rain can yield the best drawings. You must be willing to go out whatever the weather – you never know what today will bring.

Her latest passion is owning a sea kayak, so that she can explore the coastline birds and animals from sea level. Admirable. She's been out to the Bass Rock through the waves of the Forth. This is a place I'm familiar with having accompanied John Busby and his party of bird-drawers to the Bass annually for the past 17 years. We go to draw gannets and Jennie has been with us on one of these occasions. Usually the morning begins blissfully calm, an idyllic prospect ahead. Whilst out there amidst the clamour of birds, immersed in your work, you notice the sky clouding, the wind freshening and the sea getting choppy. When your boat comes to ferry you back, the weather has changed dramatically. Away from the shelter of the rock, in the full force of the wind, in black waters, slapping crests and voiding troughs concern for your own safety and that of the entire party runs through your mind. In these conditions I would fear for Jennie in her kayak.

However, Andrew, Jamie and Robyn have over the years become inured to this independent wandering spirit called 'Jennie' who is driven by some unseen force to experience and capture with paint the flora and fauna that surrounds us. In this 'nature diary', Jennie shares her love of the English countryside with us all.

David Guy Measures

APRIL 2007

Introduction

I can't remember when wildlife didn't fascinate me. It started early in childhood. I spent the first twelve years of my life in Scotland. We lived by the sea surrounded by hills so I had much to explore.

To start with, my father used to take me fishing, sometimes on the rivers for trout or salmon, sometimes to sea for mackerel. It was always exciting; chance encounters with some wild creature were always a possibility. There would be eider and scoter, gannet and cormorant around our boat, deer in the woods and wildcat in the glens. I avidly collected bugs and filled endless tanks with rock pool creatures, jam jars were filled, frogspawn collected. There were rocks and trees to climb, nests to peer into, burns to explore. When I was six a litter of pups was born under my bed and one of these wriggling bundles was going to be mine. With this pup I had a passport to explore on my own – a young girl and her dog companion left to wander and have adventures. I took to the hills, always trying to go further. When we left Scotland and finally settled in Devon, it was with this companion that I explored my new home.

This love of adventure and the encounters it provides will always live inside me. I continued to have companion dogs. Each has been a yellow Labrador and each has learnt to sit and wait while I make drawings. They have a knack of alerting me to problems and the way they move often alerts me to some creature my own senses would never pick up.

I hated school and endlessly planned escapes. I always tried to sit by the window and gazed through it constantly, longing only to be on the other side of the glass. But I did have an ability to draw, to paint and sculpt and to run like the wind from an early age and these strengths sustained me.

With these skills I went to art school to study ceramics and then to work as an assistant to Marianne de Trey, C.B.E. Eventually, I set up my own workshop in a remote and beautiful wooded valley in Devon with Andrew, my husband and father of my two children, Jamie and Robyn.

It is here that I started to write and illustrate my diaries, at first to inform my pottery and then as work in their own right. This book has been compiled from these diaries. These are some of the encounters, written or drawn, all captured with my pencils, paint or words, that nourish me and always have.

I have been lucky to travel to wild places in this country and abroad, and in each landscape, urban or wild, I see nature arrive and survive. It's that incredible spirit of survival that has always inspired my work and fuelled my sense of adventure.

January

12th January, very cold, freezing tempretures throughout the day. Every footfall is crunching, mud and leaves make the same sounds. The ground, frozen hard gives only a little, even in the thick muddy area's At the clear fell triangle a fox is sunning himself. He watches me as I rifle my bag for a pencil and paper. Not really concerned just interested. I draw until he saunters off. The deer wallow is bathed in sunshine but is frozen hard, in places so unblemished, that I poke it with a stick to see if it really is ice, it is. At the alder pond more ice with glittering patches of sunshine.

14th January. Starlings feed in the vegtable garden.
At the pond a couple of frogs pair the rest appear to be lone males. The pond is low from lack of rain.

15th January. I've been putting sunflower seeds on one of the raised beds and chaffinches arrive each day to gobble them up. I've now started putting mixed fruit and fat out for other ground feeders,

Robins, dunnocks, wagtails, a few Blackbirds and one very overfed pheasant.

27th January.

Another cold day, the birds are busy in the garden, letting me get lots of drawings done.

Blackbirds are coming in to feed they are very wary and don't like movement at the kitchen window along with them come wagtails and chaffinches. Siskins can be heard calling

as they fly over, but their not coming down to feed. There must be lots of wild food still.

28th January

Get up early to try to find where the dipper is singing. Well I find at least four places where the dipper sings. I'm not sure which is his favorite spot.

29th January Go back down and find the singing coming from the bend in the river where the trees have been felled. He singing away, then feeding and then singing again.

30 January.

Take Pumpkin out and cross the river on our log. Its another cold day but overcast.

WAXWING AT BUCKFASTLEIGH

31ST January.

The sun dips behind the hill on the far side of the river casting a beam of golden light across the estuary, turning the mud to the colour and texture of beaten copper.

The Avocets are suffused with this light as they stride across its rays.

A vast flock of widgeon take to the air and fly off to the saftey of the water. The Avocets feed on, not flying off until they haved filled their bellies or night encroaches.

My toes and fingers are now hurting with the cold and as the light goes the air chills still more.

Avocet at Weir Quay

February

8th February.

Another freezing day. I'm down in the Hams to-day by 8.15am and my reward, are two beautiful Bullfinch males nipping the buds from young oak trees on the triangle clear fell, although all around is frozen, this patch is in full sun and the birds are enjoying it. High above them a Roe moves, it's the same buck from yesterday. He's enjoying the sun and lies down to doze. I can't really see to draw from this angle so walk on, but I'll go back on the top track to see if he's still there I am delighted and surprised to find him still dozing in the sun

when I get round. What a great opperhunity to get some drawings made of him. I can't tell you how pleased I am to get this view.

9th February

Drive up to the Lake District with Nigel for our D.R.G. away trip. First thing we do is walk up to Grisdale pike on the way I hear siskins, but once we leave the trees it's only Ravens for company. My Room is good so I go out to phone Andrew. A Barn owl quarters the ground by our bunk house. I get fantastic views as it drifts across the ground and then drops into the bracken to be lost from view.

14th February. The Robins in the garden,
tolerated each other and fed together
now angrily defending
A pair hold the
Others still come
So there are some
fierce stand
offs, with much
clicking and
posturing.
who during the cold snap
around the bird table, are
their patch.
bird table area
to attempt
to feed.
BUZZARD FEATHER
REMAINS
FROM
A
SPIDERS
WEB.

Moorhens in the torch light
on Asheltor
pond.
18th February.
This morning we wake to a
flurry of snow, the weather
is very cold, but it soon turns
to slush. The Hills of Dartmoor
look magnificent in their
white cloak.
The bird table is
constantly busy.
Tonight I go down
to the pond to
look for frogs
MOORHEN ON ASHELTOR POND

A pair of Moorhen sit out in the open apart from a sparse covering of pale bare branches, one of the moorhen slinks off, but the other which woke up last stands for ages in the torchlight, a little baffled then finally swims away low in the water. A pair of mallard rise, noisely, with indignant quacks over my head.

But Frogs? I can only see three and they are way out in the pond.

Bewick Swans

March

2nd March Badger cubs at laughter hole farm.
This little boar Badger belts around and fluffs up
in mock horror and then prances around very
pleased with himself, all the time making
funny little grunts.

Badgers playing Laughter-hole farm

3rd March
Walk into the house to make some tea and what do I see? Seven hinds three of which are standing on the hedge. They browse there for about twenty minutes before moving on.
I see this group quite often at the moment, its a wonderful sight.

4th March
Ravens arrive over the house with huge beakfulls of moss. The pair make journeys to the edge of the wood, then back to the Douglas stand, they're lining their nest, this is exciting, they must have rebuilt their nest after the storm brought it down, fantastic!
As I come home across the field, I can see two raptors soaring over Langstone, one is very large.

7th MARCH

WILD DAFFODILS BY THE RIVER BELOW BAILEY BRIDGE

This morning a sparrow hawk sits on the vegtable garden fence looking at my feeding station, normally covered in small birds,

not a bird is to be seen, it sits for about 30 minutes completely unperturbed by our coming and going, I got a chance

of a couple of quick drawings before taking Robyn to her guitar lesson.
Later I head off to the river. It's still really low.
A rifle shot goes off from Longham down and then another. I doubt I'll be seeing my deer herd now. It's always like this I watch them, draw them, get used to their movements, then the hunters come, go up to the high seats and shoot them!! Anyway that's how it goes.
A Minotaur Beetle is ambling through beech leaves and pine needles at my feet, I pick him up and listen to its buzzing.

22nd March

At Kelly five lesser horseshoe bats hang by their toes in the dungeon, they are so neatly packaged.

The churchyard is awash with yellow flowers lesser celandine and Wild Daffodils. Its enchanting, thats if graveyards can be enchanting, with the ancient lichen covered tombstones, blue/grey standing amidst this joyful sea of sunshine petals, this really is. Then down on the old coach road wood anenomes appear at the sides of the track and in the more open areas more Wild Daffodils all bowing and nodding in the light breeze.

26th MARCH I've found a Buzzards nest so I have to find a good place to watch when the young hatch. 28th March North West Passage and Cut Hill.

April

18th April
I've been watching the Ravens land in the water tank coppise, I've tried to see what they're doing but I can't it must be something good. They are wonderful beasts to watch so agile and alert.
22nd April First shower of rain for two months

wood spurge

Bumble and I took a walk down the Hams tonight

it was already dark when we set off. At the gate to the second Ham owls started to call the one nearest me sounded like an old asthmatic, wheezing and snorting its call, even in flight it wheezed out its call.

It's very peaceful here in the dark I like to watch Bumble, she sits in front of me but her ears are pricked and nose held high listening to the night noises its funny the way her chest puffs out. While I sit she won't move from my side. Heading home we get to the blackthorn patch when the wood erupts with sound, somethings directly behind the blackthorn lots of crackling of dry leaves, I wait knowing that what

ever's making the noise might appear in the field or if the noise goes then, I'll think it's Badgers returning home very noisily.

I don't have to wait long, for not ten yards from me first two then three red deer step warily in to the open, they stand on the track listening for any danger their large mobile ears flicking forwards and back straining for sounds. The wind's in my favour so is the darkness the moon gives just enough light for me to watch them settle and start to graze. Dark forms moving against the pale grasses.

BLACKTHORN FROM JAYS THICKET

25th April. While we sit gazing at the newts and tadpoles, red deer venture across the coppice by the water tank and quietly browse on new leaves. The sun's hot to-day and Jamie and I doze in the heat beside the pond. 6:30pm Bumble and I set off to walk around the valley again. The light is good and the birdsong wonderful.

Everywhere I look bird activity is at its height Residents feeding young, migrants building nests, chacking of blackcaps, squabbles of Jays and an irate group of small birds babbling angrily after a sparrowhawk. At my nestboxes I wait a while to see who's using them, to my delight a pied flycatcher is feeding nearby and then darts into the nestbox. She repeats this again and again. Excellent! Now that the track has been pushed through, the area has been opened up and offers lots and lots of hunting perches

The pond has got masses and masses of pondweed, King cups spread back up into the clearing with areas of larch. It's a good time to be out tonight, every now and then I feel a warm gust of breeze on my face. The railway track feels very open compared with last year surrounded by all the clear fell.

But it's still sheltered by the hill, the trees are not quite out and their canopy is turning subtle hues of pink, ochre and green. The colour floods through the tops changing the landscape daily. Below wood anenomes and wood sorrel flower. Primroses turn the ground lemon yellow, amid this violets stand like bright little eyes in a carpet of pale colours. The Bluebells not quiet fully out tinge the ground with their purple/blue soon the earth will disappear beneath this lapis cloak. The sun warms and wakes the land.

May

6th May
Hobbys hunting bats and insects they are giving a similar call to the one they give when they are feeding their young. Saw both together along with two Buzzards soaring, I could clearly see the size difference between the sexes in the Hobbys. They fly until the light has gone; their flying is spectacular at the moment.

10th May. Went down to the Badger sett in the first Ham and watched a Badger excavating. The digging was so vigorous that clods of earth were flying down the slope to me, I was sitting about thirty feet away!

11th May went back to the sett tonight to see how the work was progressing. The same Badger was now collecting leaves 3/4 of an hour later still busy collecting leaves, then three other Badgers sett off foraging totally ignoring the one doing all the work.

Barn owl feathers.

13th May
Went down to the barn in the marshy field. A Tawny owl has nested in the huge old willow stump outside the barn, watched this youngster in the entrace hole did a couple of sketches using the telescope, so as not to disturb it, the adults were in the far hedge calling softly.
Found the Barn owl feathers under a roost amongst lots of fresh droppings

Went down to the river to have a look at another Badger sett. There were some signs of life but not a lot.

Young Tawny owl in Willow stump.

puppies for twenty minutes. Then as one dissappear towards the earth.
I think an adult has returned with food.
Waited a while longer for them to return, but no luck, still, what a view I've had.
I can hear the deer and the badger moving across the hill below me, I ought to go home now, the light has completely gone.

18th May walked upto the high ground to see if the foxes are about and have been rewarded by wonderful views of three well grown fox cubs, playing tag in the bluebells and bracken, they pounce, wiggle pounce again, then scratch thier fleas, pull at each others ears and tails , playing like

Badger cub foraging
below Longham
Down.
Jamie has left
his window open to allow the bats
into his bedroom, lesser horseshoe
bats come in and hang upside down
on his curtain rail above his bed.
It looks as if they're having a bat party.

Eider ducks

22nd May
Bastard Balm flowers on the track.

23rd May Pearl bordered fritillaries flit among the Bluebells above the Alder pond. Small coppers bask in the sunshine. At the deerwallow a male broad bodied chaser is zooming around, every now and then coming into land on the soft rush.

24 May Beesands

I got down to Beesands with Dad, Robyn and Fudgie, its very lush, patches of thrift bloom near the beach. The ley is surrounded by dense foliage. Tufted duck about seven in all scoot about in the distance, close by a great crested grebe hunts for aquatic prey, it looks so sleek and beautiful in its breeding plumage, at the edge of a field lurks a heron, another on the edge of the reed bed and the clockwork movements of coot and moorhen fragment the surface of the water.

Robyn and I search for shells and find some interesting ones on the beach. On the way back to dad's we stop at Strete gate to draw the sea campion.

Its pretty down here, I'd forgotton how much I used to like to come here.

Back home and down the valley

Green veined white on cuckoo flower roosting, the Green veined whites like to roost on the flowers near the wallow, lots of cuckooflower in bloom.

At the forest pond kingcups have gone over but the yellow flags are not yet out.

Still no Toad poles to be seen, what's happened?

Everything moves so fast at this time of year it's hard to keep up with it all. Towards the Butterfly reserve vetch blooms, its such a wonderful colour, magenta and blue, a jewel, bugle flowers profusly all along the reserve and by the edges cow wheat send tiny yellow heads into the sedge and grasses. Tadpoles at the drain pool, growing steadily larger. No sign of newts.

26 May Oil beetles glinting turquoise blue in the sun engrossed in munching lesser celandine, they are strange looking creatures, the females are huge with enlarge abdomens, they look edible!!

June

Bastard Balm longham track.
1ST June
A small pearl bordered fritillary
feeding on Bugle.
I was chasing Butterflies for a better view when I saw a hind lying in the grass dozing, so I sat to watch her, it's near calving time, I'm interested to see where they go now.

Buzzard Feather

She sat snoozing for a while then opened her eyes, all I could see of her was part of her neck and head appearing over the bracken that was newly merged and the bluebells, the sun

Variable Longhorn Beetle.

to the touch, it fascinates me.

On the hill home, cowwheat in bloom, a thick covering of cowwheat and Bilberry. Soft calling from Hobby.

8th June Rain Blustery.

Up to the high ground again the rain soaked vegatation has my trousers saturated in minutes, its showery and windy.

In the Redwoods a glade of columbines look lovely in this light the blue almost glows, but the wind makes them impossible to draw.

made shadows dance across her face when she moved, I think she picked up my scent for she was at once alert, rose, stretched and slowly moved away, delicately picking her way through the gorse.

I went to see where she had lain, the grasses flattened in a medium sized oval, a few flattened Blue bells nothing more, the ground just slightly warmer

Wasp Beetle

Wild STRAWBERRIES ON THE TRACK TO THE FIRST HAM

Gatekeeper

15th June

Rescued a young wood mouse this morning and after feeding and watering, it repaid me by being an artists model for the morning. A delightful little creature. It seemed quite at home eating niger seed and drinking from an egg cup.

16th June

Go for a walk this evening and meet a newly fledged nest of Jays. They are very entertaining, not able to fly properly, they lept from tree to tree grabing hold of twigs with their beaks, flapping and walking up branches, four of them flapped and hopped trying to gain hieght so they

Could tumble to the next tree.

By the forest pond a small pale gold moth pendulumes in a shallow arch above the grasses. I watch fascinated by this display, a ghost moth in its courtship dance.

21st June

It's incredibly windy today

A warm wind heated by some unseen land and with it comes the migrant moths and Butterflies, the garden now has a resident population of silver-y-moths and Hummingbird hawkmoths zap around breaking the insect speed limit as they go into hyperdrive.

FEATHERS FROM A GREAT SPOTTED WOODPECKER.

Field vole

Lesser Butterfly orchid
Sylvias Field
HEATH SPOTTED ORCHID.

Southern Marsh orchid

24th June
The wallow is drying out but the marshy area is still very wet. I spend an hour drawing Ragged Robin, the thick scent of peppermint fills my nostrils from the plants crushed under my feet. A Southern Marsh orchid blooms all alone in the grass, will more appear. Across the river in Daves steep field a hind stands, I watch her large ears dredge the breeze, then I see what she has beside her, a new born calf, the first I've seen this year it's lying in the grass, the hinds belly looks saggy, she stands licking her calf and listening for any danger.

At the forest pond Damselflies Asure and large red stick from the water's surface like a forest of tiny iridescences.

Some lift from the surface, coupled or singly to fly on those flimsy wings to the Alders or Yellow flags to rest.

After a while we drift up to the Roman fort area on North long ridge. More grizzled skippers on the track. Then on the Roman fort Small pearl bordered Fritillary in abundance everywhere we look, lots are flying

it's lovely here. I haven't been here for a while, when Jamie was a toddler I spent lots of time up here with him looking for bugs. At that time the small pearl bordered where on the far slope which was covered in bracken but is now covered in larch.

There's a lovely caterpillar resting on a Bluebell, a Red Chesnut moth caterpillar

After a while we walk up to the High ground.

A Tawny owl is being pursued by small birds, it flies along the bottom track only to be driven back and into the christmas trees.

July

SILVER WASH FRITILLARY ON KNAPWEED

3rd July Heard the squeaky hinge hiccup call that the Hobbys give as a recognition call, often to last years young, when I was out in the garden.

For a week now Andrew and I have been hearing a squeaky mewing - a bit like a young Buzzard but not that.

To-day I went to see if there was anything happening at the Hobbys nest and found the makers of that call, Three possibly four young sparrow hawks all branching around their nest site. The wood was vibrating with their cries a sort of squeally mew.

They flit from tree to tree and call as they wait for a parent to come with food; the parent birds were feeding constantly all afternoon, I was there for three and a half hours.

The young fly well but their landsare haphazard, the often misjudged the twigs that they landed on and fell off.

They are all well grown only one had an odd bit of down on its back.

Young SPARROWHAWK IN LIPSCLIFFE WOOD

But they all had areas of white feathers on their backs.

I can see the nest, it's covered in droppings and there are lots of feathers around it.

I think I'll go back and collect some later.

I went down to the Hams tonight on the way down two deer crossed the track in front of me, I've seen the deer runs down on that steepside and I knew it was well used, but I've not seen them there before. They look huge as they come down from above me onto the track.

4th July The Hobbys are holding a new territory, they've been very secretive this year, calling only after dark. Great catch in the moth trap lots of Jolly Garden Tigers and Poplar Hawkmoths

5th July
Another good catch Privet and Poplar Hawkmoths in same numbers, a Shark and Green Arches.
THE Hobbys are calling tonight 7.30pm.
We've had so much rain it feels like spring or Autumn, cold and wet. Will the sun ever come out !!
6th July The baby Swallows have just left their nest and are sitting in a neat row on one rafter, pale versions of the Adults.

7th July Haldon Forest with Robin Khan to see nightjars

Robin phoned this morning to say it should be good for nightjars tonight, so I was up at Haldon for 9 p.m. A lovely still evening.

We went to what Robin calls Nightjar City. As the light dimmed churring could be heard in the distance then a male bird flew up and landed in the new growth in front of us, more churring further up the track towards the silver birch. We walked quietly up towards the silver birch and found ourselves in the centre of Nightjar activity, first a displacement display overhead, then a female lands on the track right in front of us, trying to lure away from her nest site.

8th July In an isolated pond I find Broad bodied chaser nymphs and Damselfly nymphs.

12th July Meadowsweet and Ragged Robin flower in the marsh.
I've just found some dragonfly wings, they glitter in the light.
As I stand drawing in the marsh the air cools, it's 10pm and I'm standing in a river mist, but as soon as I climb from the marsh the heat returns only to disappear as I walk to lower ground. The mist has formed in all the hollows and pockets of low marshy ground.
A bright yellow orbweb spider lands on my hand, her abdomen like a bright colourful marble.
At the clearfell triangle, first I hear the deer then I see one moving uphill, she's watching some thing further up, it's a second hind and a young calf, the calf moves close to its mother and all three move off up the hill in silence.
14th July common sandpiper at

COMMON SANDPIPER

RINGLET WING FROM A SPIDERS WEB.

DRAGONFLYWINGS.

Ashel tor pond, resting on the bridge. It slept for some time then woke, stretched and returned to sleep. A moorhen chirrups across the pond followed a few moments later by four fluffy chicks all flustered by the open water.

Buzzard chick

COMMON BLUES ON RAGGED ROBIN

14th July Another muggy hot day. The silver wash fritillaries are out big, bright and fresh, they dash from bramble blossom to bramble blossom feeding.

20th July
Walked miles this evening. The different areas of the forest have different scents. In the conifers the sap smells sweet and spicy, then the damp loamy valley and the sultry rich honeysuckle, a smell so thick I feel I should be able to swallow it.
North longridge is well grown with larch. The little path down, steep but not as churned as last time.
I'm high above the valley bottom, well hidden by the new growth, looking down on a pair of Roe deer, in the fading light the colour of their coats seems to glow, tiny faces, such slender legged fairy creatures, they browze on the shrubs. I watch them slowly drift away from me, feeding then sniffing the air finally moving into the cover by the river.

24th July

Jamie returned home with Beautiful Demoiselles and a Gold ringed Dragonfly for me to draw, he's had a great time with the butterflynet.

We went back later to release them and found small skippers. Then went to collect some cinnabar caterpillars.

There are hundreds of ladybird larvae and pupae on the nettles and christmas trees. We brought a pupae home and it hatched out in the night. Much excitement.

Common Centaury growing in the second Ham, fragrant Agrimony in the hedge and masses of wood sage.

27th July Tremendous thunder and lightening storm, the sky was ablaze and the thunder made me bounce with fright.

Goldringed DRAGONFLY

Large Skipper

26th July
Great excitement this evening when Jamie noticed the Oleander Hawkmoth pupaes had hatched, he was dancing up and down. They are spectacular, one is brighter green than the other but both are exquisite.
As each day goes by there are more butterflies down at the pump.
I found some more fragrant Agrimony it has a wonderful spicy smell.

28th July. Cinnabar caterpillars on the rag wort in the second Ham. There was a Badger in the forest by the clear felling, it seemed to have longer legs than normal, I expect it was the angle that I was looking from.
Further on a hind was grazing by the path her back towards me as she grazed, there's three of them, as they loped off I could see those large feet and they're gone.

Eyed hawk moth

30th July On the way home I stop to look at the Hams. Two Red deer browse by the hedge. It's then I see a badger, first one then another and another eventually five all feeding on the bright green grass, lots of light so they are easy to watch. I'm busy watching them, when, what could possibly be a fox starts to pace the fence line, head held low at a funny angle, it's a Roe buck, looks as if he's sniffing along the fence line, sometimes running, often just pacing up and down, then

MOORHEN ASHELTOR POND

a dash to the hedge and back right over the top of a Badger who's having a good scratch.

Now the Red deer have joined the Roe buck in the field, but he just continues his low headed pacing.

A noise at my feet makes me look down two feet away is a Badger cub, he comes under the gate right beside me, scent marks then drops into the stream for a drink!

BADGER AND CUB LONG HAM.

August

2nd August Kennack sands. snorkelling.
Towards the shore Ballan Wrasse of all sizes drift amongst the kelp.

Two-spot Blennies surge with the tide above the seaweed, large and small all feeding together on the incoming tide.

A few pollock swiftly move past.
Among the kelp are many different coloured algae bright scarlet pink, vivid greens, rich reds and rusts, strange pink crusts spread across boulders, coral weed bunches sprout from the rocks, wonderful snakelock anenomos blossom beneath the waves their tangle of tentecles floating in the surge.

There's a wide variety of anenomes in the pools, beadlet and others all cramed on to barnacle encrusted rocks. I have a lovely time holding on to the rocks or a handful of kelp to anchor me then watching the barnacles fanning out to feed

or just drifting up and down with the tiny fish.

A pair of velvet swimming crabs, the male carrying the female huddle beneath a rock fending off my attempts to pick them up.

The male will carry the female when she is almost ready to cast her shell then they can mate, so he carries her around with him.

Crossing the bay I pass through curtains of glittering sand eels and swim over foraging shore crabs as the tide floods everything comes out to feed.

A small dab flickers in front of me one moment undulating along the next almost invisable in the sand.

At the eastern end of the bay the water is clear and deep. I drift between boulders and jutting rocks large silver fish swim past, they look like Bass, then a solitary deep silver one with glittering Stripes, could that be a Black Sea-bream or oldwife, more bass drift past me over the rocks.

15th August Heathers in colourful carpets stretch away from me, I looked for Bilberries but couldn't find any, it's been so dry the flowers probably didn't set. I found some Fox moth caterpillars and watched Southern Hawkers whizzing about on the tracks through the woods.

19th August
Small copper feeding on ice plants in the garden. Hobbys calling at dusk.

20th August We've got common darters in the garden zooming about and small copper, tortoishell, Red admiral and lots of large and small whites The flower borders are festooned with silver-y-moths and butterflies, each of them flickering up and down in the sun. The whole effect is mesmerizing and sometimes I find I've been standing gazing at it all for ages. Certain butterflies choose a particular flower to visit each day, the small copper on the sedum and the common blue on the bright

FOX MOTH CATERPILLAR

pointed under the table she was quite right, a beautiful young grass snake was zigzagging towards her across the flagstones, so now it's been released into the garden much to Robyn's delight.

yellow Rudebeckia

22nd August
We're gathering up the grass snake hatchling, escapes, one under a shoe, one in a shoe and today one under the table.
Robyn at twenty months old asked for a drink, then whe she got it yelled "shnaake shnaake" and

The fading butterflies remind me of a wedding tree, whose bright gaudy scarves after summers and winters of fluttering, turn into tattered fragments that move with the winds, like these tiny tattered fragments that move around me now.

A pair of squirrels come constantly into the garden to gobble up my birdfood and destroy my feeders.

23rd August
Hobbys calling above Brandis wood.
Convolvulus Hawkmoths zooming over the garden.
I watched two tonight zipping about, I was hoping they might feed on the tobacco plants, but the were busy flying around. They always make me think of flying saucers when they fly, one minute in one direction and then, away as if blown by a sudden gust of wind in the other, all at incredible speed like little U.F.O.S.

24th August. NO MOON LOTS OF STARS.
Hobby calling.
Convolvulus Hawkmoths zooming around.
It rained last night the first rain in weeks.

GRASS SNAKE HATCHLINGS.

25th August
Butterflies flit around the garden in colourful clouds, comma and small copper on the Rubeckia, red admiral and peacocks on buddliea and thousands of whites; all flitting around with masses of silver y moths.

27th August
Walk from Poolewe
to Loch
Maree

A track about eight
K'ms long which
runs down the side
of Loch Maree.
to start with, the
sundews grow on the edge.

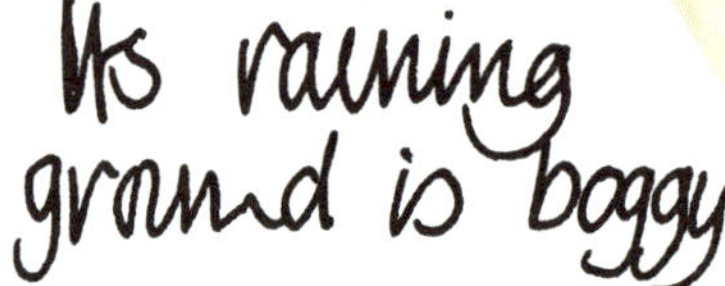

Its raining
ground is boggy

Bumble Bee on Teasle by our gate.

Sexton Beetle from the moth trap.

29th August

Hobby calling loudly outside it sounds as if it's coming from the oak tree by our track gate.
It's in the air circling the tree then lands at the top of an Ash tree right in front of me, sits there blinking while being mobbed by swallows. Another Hobby flies over, trying to encourage its youngster to get out of the tree and away from the angry swallows.

30th August.
Coots paddle across the lake, sending ripples over the surface to turn the perfectly mirrored sticks and reeds into fragments that thread across the water.
Towards the back of the inlet Teal feed in a small group these are such flighty little ducks, so pretty and oh, so, wild.
Off shore a lone Cormorant fishes, its elongated silhouette seems more snaked necked in this low light.

September

6th September

I can hear deer moving and spot them above me.

The hollow I'm in is deep and dark so they can scent me but it's not too disturbing, four or five hinds all have their calves up there in the Hollies Sunlight streams in on their flanks lighting them with strong shadows.

Small patches of blue sky are scattered down one side, the light highlights the sloping trunks of some trees.

The hinds wander above me alert and tense. The calves pick up their mother's tension and walk around stiff legged.

Soon they move away but I have snatched a drawing today.

8th September.
A vixen's carrying a rabbit across the hill below me.
I try squeaking, she stops and listens but isn't interested so quickly moves on. I think I'm going to have to practise this, it's hot today.

9th September
Young Roe buck just down from the deep track, it's like a spring ready to bounce away but curiosity keeps it there, trying to make something of my bent form.
Bumbles' return sends its head lower and finally it takes flight towards dense cover.

DEVIL'S-BIT SCABIOUS

12th September It's rained and rained for the last two days. But today the sun is up and I'm woken by the kek! kek! kek! of a young Hobby on his first flight across the valley. The youngster is accompanied by an adult who flies with ease around the very fluttery young bird. It's touchingly comic, very like Jamie learning to swim panicky flapping and fluttering in the water, they fly over the house and back again, doing lengths.

15th September
Humming bird Hawkmoth in the garden feeding.

16th September
Humming bird Hawkmoth again.

21st September

Well after yesterday I will have to change my route, so I cross the river and climb onto the Butterfly reserve. I forgot how beautiful it is. The oak woods behind are dappled with slanting light, the columns of their trunks thick with antiquity, below the canopy little grows so the ground is carpeted in leaf litter.

A new sett has been opened up near the embankment, maybe a good place to view from. Yellow Hawksbit and Devils bit scabious bloom on the first sector. Then on the third sector I watch a red admiral lazily drift down the bank, its bright colours glittering above the faded straws of the grasses. The passing of this butterfly causes small coppers to rise from the grass; they burst into the air spinning like dervishes, tumbling fragments that flicker brown and orange in the light. Their hectic dance spins and twirls as they spiral up and then dash across the sward. Black and Ruddy darters quarter the ground.

The sun is warm with a warm breeze.
I see the summer ebbing but the warmth remains.

KNOBBER AND HIND.

22nd September
This morning is warm still and overcast. The woods seem quiet after yesterdays clattering breeze. Ravens call as do raucous Jays.
At the bailey bridge small salmon move across the stream bed their thumb print markings easy to see in this light; Brown trout dart ever fearful, the explode from one dark corner to another.
The lack of rain has made the river half its normal size, the river waits now for autumn storms to bring new life into its arteries. In fact this morning it feels as if the whole forest valley is waiting
23rd Cotehele River Tamar 5.30 p.m.
The tide is flooding and pushing hard up the river. It will be fun to paddle on a big tide.
The river takes us along at a fair lick, we've soon left the quay behind and are moving steadily up stream. A salmon leaps right by my paddle I suddenly saw its face appear out of

COMMA

the muddy water it really makes me jump, more salmon jump further up river from us, some are very large, its very exciting to see their silver shapes arch from the water. As the days move towards October more and more will be gathering and waiting for the rain that will give them access to the river above the weirs.

Above Calstock a tern catches my eye, it bobs and dips as it flies along, a Black tern in autumn moult a delightful little bird, up and down the river it goes, passing over the canoe serval times. I'm busy watching this when a peregrine appears from the Devon bank, soars over head, across the reedbeds

to Cornwall. In moments a loud series of cries goes up as a very angry sparrowhawk tries to drive the Peregrine away. The peregrine moves out of the way effortlessly as the ruffled sparrowhawk pursues its foe, while constantly giving aggressive alarm calls, soon the peregrine returns to Devon's riverbank and the calm returns.

The tide is still rising and we're so past Morwellham, upstream towards the weir, ducks rise from the banks, I see the first of the winter's teal, that during the cold months of the year populate the river. It grows slowly darker and finally with about 300 meters to go before the weir our way is blocked by a river full of debris.

We turn and paddle back down stream. The calls from the banks have now changed as the night takes over, Tawny owls make their contact calls. The leaping salmon now just loud splashes, the rising of duck the whirring of wings and water movement as they rise from the river.
Above our heads the soft wash of the Milkyway draps itself above the river.

I spend my time gazing at the stars and paddle silently through the dark, the calm of the river descends and all that can be heard is the movement of water against the hull of the canoe.

28th September.
Gold ringed Dragonfly, Common Darter and Migrant Hawkers all down in the Christmas tree clearing. I can hear the Gold ringed as it sits on a twig crunching the flies its caught.

31st September.
The hedges are full of Autumnal Jumble, convolvulus and vetch scramble over the ferns and grasses, Guelder rose and Elder laden with succulent berries bow towards the ground, each day brings richer colours to natures palette as the leaves begin to turn.
In Coles wood high above me a hind browses, I'll have to get near her to draw her.

October

7th October.
Daily walks around Brandiz wood have
only given brief sightings of deer. But
the wallows are getting used and
judging by the slots, the deer
are about but I'm not seeing them.
9th October
Cave spiders. The spring has
six spider egg sacks hanging
from the ceiling and
some large female spiders

but the second tank has twelve nests. Sticking my head in the hole to take a look is a bit alarming as I usually end up, eyeball to eyeball with an enormous female cave spider! It's worth it just to see such an array of dangling nests decorating the dark tanks. The females abdomens are fat and a rich ochre, rust on top, dark below, the males, I've looked at are a mixture of dark and light browns and lots of small spiderlings in grey brown hues.

10th October
Fox in Brandiz wood, pretty little pointed face and no tag, she moves off as soon as she sees me.
David says the foxes are chittering and calling.

Cave SPIDER

He's heard frogs croaking he's the second person to mention that.

13th October.

More and more Deer activity in Brandis Wood. The cut across the deep track is heavily used. At the top the muddy rut has tracks over my footprints, Red Deer and Badger today, precise slots and those small round toes with claw points of the Badger. There is something reassuring in the way their tracks cover mine. Coryhill plantation has a fox at the bottom, small with no tag, my squeaking brought her closer to me, but she's not sure. I'll have to work on my technique.

15th October Great Staple Tor large flock of Golden plover swirl in the air, silver then gold as the sun caught their backs, shimmering wave of birds dipping away in the distance.

Sitting looking out at Great Mis Tor a sudden flurry of small birds, alerts me to a merlin, who flies in and lands below on the granite clitter, pipits rush in every direction. Then moments later its off flying low and fast around the tor scattering linnets in its wake. I scramble round and find a recent kill amid the rocks.

17th October It's rained.

The woods are damp and musty smelling it's a lovely earthy scent. Each day the carpet of leaves thickens in the deep track, ochres, browns and yellows with diffrent nuts spread over them.

FEATHERS FROM A MERLIN KILL

Tattered Tortoishell wings

SWEET CHESTNUT

21st October

Redwings and fieldfare feed in the ditches. They look jolly. Each evening they fly over the house to roost in the Sitka plantation.

22nd October

A Badger night for sure. First of all Jamie Robyn and I see one on the road by Ashel tor, then at the barn six Badgers are feeding together. Jamie and Robyn were really excited leaping from their seats for a better view.

The Badgers appear to be in a large family group, some youngsters with adults.

Then when I returned to the barn 15 minutes later three Badgers are feeding there.

And then one and a half hours later on my way home two more Badgers are feeding. Good worm feast maybe!

Hawthorn Berries

23rd October
Chaffinch flocks are appearing whereever the beech trees are, and today I see a white flash of rump, a Brambling.

Toing and froing to Liddaton tonight has brought me lots of Badger views. Robyn now calls the bottom of our lane Badger World.

Autumn Brambles

Each time I went past the barn Badgers trundled in all directions, all going busily on their foraging trips.

24th October 5:30 am.
Up and out early to get to a rutting stand before dawn. I can hear roaring as I walk towards the stand, through conifer

then oak, the track leads towards the roars, bellows echo all around, this is from a fair sized beast, as yet unseen but the bass note and volume tell me this is a large stag. At the clearing that is the rutting stand four hinds stand edgy, the wind now over my right ear, carries my scent, but they stay.

A stag bursts from cover, charges towards the christmas trees, sending hinds scattering as he disappears into the trees. A pricket enters the clearing his body, youthful, slender and adolescent in comparison. He seems confused by the excited hinds, the roaring and the hormone fuelled drama.

25th October
The berries are stripped from the hedge in front of the workshop, I watch the blackbirds arrive and wobble down spindley twigs to reach succulant fruits they crane forward to grab them and gobble them down.

30th October.
It's rained hard for two days now and for the first time in months the river has risen, it's the colour of tea and I am sure after all this waiting the Salmon will be running.

So I head straight to the river bank to look, the pool the children swim in has had the over hanging trees felled so it's now an open sunny pool.
With the extra water it's too murky to see anything. I'll go up stream.

November

24th NOVEMBER WHOOPER SWANS WELNEY

It's a long drive back from Norfolk, made worse by the rain. At Bridestow the road is completely flooded, water laps over the bonnet of my landrover as I drive slowly through, headlights dim submerged, its eerie and seems

to take ages to get through. By the time I get near home it's 12:30am and near the bottom of the hill I know I won't get home tonight, the river has burst its banks, the bridge and railings are under water, I reverse wearily up the road and try to wake people in the nearest house, NO GOOD! I begin to think I'll be out all night, when I think of someone who might be up and yes he is, so I get to sleep on his sofa!!

25th November

Thurshes and Blackbirds are everywhere I look in the woods, rooting through the dry leaves, more come into the garden to feed, enjoying the rotten apples. The garden feeding places are attracting large numbers of birds; the band of coal tits often bring a tiny bright goldcrest with them. These generally work the vegetables for morsels and don't go to the easy pickings of the birdtable.

26th November It's very cold this morning but so far dry, then after my walk

it starts to snow and snow within 30 minutes the ground is completely covered in snow and after an hour the yard is thick with snow. The whole valley is a winter landscape of exquisite beauty The only thing is the

children are at school and we have to get them home. The school transport has suspended services. Thank god for our landy, Andrew managed to get them home.

They are very excited and spend the rest of the day sledging down the hill to the river.

27th November

Still lots of snow and more sledging the roads have frozen over, so now we have hard packed ice.

Walk up through the frost covered field and woods, snow lies on the ground transforming my familiar landscape.

All the nights activities are printed on the ground, the dainty slots of Roedeer, the much larger ones of Red.

A fox, neat prints the hind print on the front, and snout marks where some tasty morsel has been found.

Young stag

28th November
Coming home I get a rare look at a Stoat. They often are just blurs but this one was hunting and had jumped onto the track in front of me, for moments he was intent on his quarry, but then realize he wasn't alone and darted off in a blur of movement. Fantastic! They are lovely little murderers.
The whole episode is accompanied by the sound of a hind belly grunting at me, when I turn to go above me on the hillside stand six deer all looking down and the lead hind grunts on.
8.30pm Along from West Liddaton a Barn owl banks over the road, I haven't seen one there for ages, does this mean they may be in one of the barns again?

29th November Bowling green Marsh
Although the tide is high the marsh dosen't have huge numbers of birds, Shelduck at one end and a few Shoveler, Blacktailed Godwit, Dunlin, Redshank and a solitary Avocet all close together on the edge of the island. Wigeon and teal dabble on the edges of the water. A moorhen scutters across the ditch in front of me.

The hedges by the road are full of redwing and greenfinch feeding.

From the bank of the river there are good views of the estuary. The tide is high and two cormorants sit on sentry duty on an old barge.

Over by the reeds a little egret dances up and down, first rushing one way then darting off in the opposite direction.

30th November
A Pheasant comes regularly into the garden he's bright and exotic.
I see hen pheasants in the lane but they don't come in to the garden. They do seem to sulk

around and keep to cover
Blackbirds, male birds with dark beaks and dark rings around their eyes have arrived in the woods and garden, these are migrant birds who join the brightly beaked birds that are resident here.
Chaffinches have arrived in large numbers, the males again are flushed with diffrent hues, some are rosey pink and others a distinct rusty pink, again its migrant birds joining the residents.
It's a still morning, deer seem to be moving all around Longham woods, their nights activity

KESTRAL IN THE CLEAR FELL BELOW BOTTERFLY RESERVE

traced in the soft mud and that thick musky scent that clings to the brush. A tiny treecreeper works its way up the north side of the trees where moss and lichen grows it bobs its way higher and higher, then tumbles like a falling leaf to the bottom of the next tree, constantly probing for morsels.

December

12th December
Driving back from Tavistock in the dark, I notice what looked like a white handkerchief in the trees. As I got nearer, a little heart shaped face turned and looked over its shoulder. A Barn owl, looking glitteringly white against the black sky.

16th December
This evening as I cross the ford a seatrout flicks around in the shallows of the stream, then even though only half covered with water wriggles across the ford and slips in to a pool, its flanks

were well marked with blotches shaped like primroses, a good sized fish.

18th December 8a.m on the river Tamar.

There's a heavy mist and the river has a mysterious quality, ghostly shapes of moored yachts loom in and out of view, we paddle upstream to where the geese and redshank feed opposite Holes Hole, the sun starts to break through, the river is like a mirror, not a breath of wind. Common Sandpiper and kingfisher reflect perfectly in the water its completely exquisite, as duck fly up their shapes flicker back from the surface of the river

20th December

A cold sunny morning with wintery showers. Huge vivid rainbows swoop over the valley, dark storm clouds, steel grey. with slanting sun illuminate the rainbows vibrant colours. The garden is busy with birds all coming to feed at the bird tables. My resident Cock pheasant feeds and then preens himself in the sunshine. Great spotted woodpecker fly in and out. Crow and magpie, always wary snatch morsels when they think no-ones looking. Robins, greenfinches, dunnock all feed on the ground, Great, Blue, Coal and marsh tit flit to and fro grabbing beakfulls then zipping off to eat in some hidden corner. I spend the morning watching and drawing marvelling at their shapes and colours. The cold morning brings so many at once

This afternoon Pumpkin and I cross the river into the Sitka stand, Red deer are at the far side, the glimpsed me but haven't yet moved off. I crouch low and wait, they settle and start to browse, a knobber and four hinds. The stags neck is shaggy but not thick, the hinds seem calm and move towards me, then stop and look north, some distant noise has drawn their attention. I watch them moving through the trees until they dissappear into the valley of Chapel Ham, their passage through the woods, just a few twig snaps and the movement of undergrowth.

By the time I get into the second Ham it's nearly dark, redwings which have been flying overhead for some time now are settling down for the night in the dense foliage of the Christmas trees, the trees are crackling with their calls thousands of birds have gathered all calling and muttering their own thrush night fall chatter, squawks and squabbles rumble deep into the blackness of the trees, these normally silent conifers are now noisey as any nightclub.

21ST December BOWLING GREEN MARSH

Waders roost and ducks feed, the wigeon are joined on the grass by lapwing and a few golden plover, in amongst them are boisterous starlings jumping and hopping through the throng of birds. The Blacktailed Godwits and Avocets have been joined by Bartailed Godwits, the tide is very high today and the Bartailed can no longer feed until the water recedes a bit. The Marsh is busy with the activities of the day, feeding

AVOCETS BY THE GOATWALK TOPSHAM.

preening and displaying from the teal. There are thousands of birds here, then in an instance the whole scene is transformed as every bird takes to the air, a sheet of glittering colour and movement rises as if drawn by an invisible string, the culprit, a Peregrine streaks across the marsh at hedge height, sending every bird into a frantic bundle of feathers fleeing for it's life. The Peregrine makes another pass and then lands in a bare tree silhouetted against the sky. The sun, very bright today, brands the image of the Peregrine and branches on to the sky.

With the Peregrine sitting sentinal on that tree, the waders and ducks land but the flocks are vigilant, taut with anxiety, they can't settle to feed or rest.

Then in seperate flocks, first the Godwits then the Avocets lift and drift over the bank to the river, where the tide has dropped to enable them to feed.

22nd December
In the Sitka Siskins whiz about.
Dawlish Warren. Hide hide.
When I arrive at the bay Brent Geese near the beach feeding in the shallow water.
I head for the hide to watch the Oystercatchers.

23rd December. Lapwings feeding in Ed Blowey's fields near Broadpark. More Redwing in the coppice today. Lots of signs of Badger digging, found a beautiful oak apple, very red and green.

The pond is half frozen and not a thing moves up here, I check for Otter spraint under the bridge and am delighted to find a new deposit, fantastic full of little bones, treasure!!

Starlings on the Bird table

A vixen often comes into the field to find morsels, where the cattle have lain all night, today she is skittering like a puppy in the snow, pouncing and snuffing her nose in then tossing her head or stalking magpies she has no hope of catching
25 December

The woods are noisy in the wind, some of the gusts are very strong crashing the branches into each other, I head for the High ground through the Redwoods, A hind thunders out of the deep track beside me, I was upon her before she

Bren tor church from Brandiz Wood.

knew, my footfalls hidden in the wind. She's turned towards me, three trees away but with my back to the Redwoods she can't make me out, so she stands bunched ready for flight. It's growing dark as I reach the High ground but it's beautiful and wild in this riotous wind, I can just make out the curves of the valley below.